In *This Voice Has an Echo*, Emma McCoy calls on us to take time, to listen quietly, to allow her verses to resound in our own creative hearing. We respond not just to the words on the pages of this adventurous new collection, but to affirm how our own hearing takes and grows as we delight in the voice of a kindred spirit. This is just what such fresh writing will do, allowing the biblical characters to develop three-dimensional authenticity as they hear what their own voices are announcing, describing, or imagining.
—**LUCI SHAW,** author of *An Incremental Life*

What an incredible full-length debut from Emma McCoy! *This Voice Has an Echo* takes a deep dive into the lives of the prophets (including the oft-excluded women). Drawing from both Christian and Jewish traditions, McCoy matches prophetic voices with a variety of poetic forms, sometimes setting the prophets in their original contexts, and sometimes placing them in new situations or updating their dialects. The result is surprising, delightful, thought-provoking, and brilliant. Set aside whatever you think you'll find in this book, and let these poems call you out or call you in.
—**KATIE MANNING,** editor-in-chief of *Whale Road Review*

I like the poet's engagement with Scripture—to expound, to imagine, to associate, to make contemporary, as Ehud in a bar and Miriam at the Blackfoot River in Montana. McCoy writes of the lesser prophets, Haggai, Habakkuk, Amos, Obadiah, Joel. She addresses the more familiar names, Elijah, Job, Daniel, Isaiah, the Lord himself. She writes of the women, Sarah, Abigail, and Deborah in sonnet form. I was glad to meet them all.
—**DIANE GLANCY,** author of *Psalm to Whom(e)*

THIS VOICE HAS AN ECHO

EMMA McCOY

THIS VOICE HAS AN ECHO

Emma McCoy

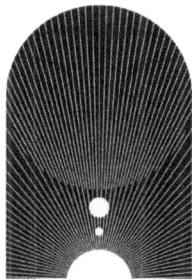

SOLUM
LITERARY PRESS

Scottsdale, AZ • solumpress.com

Solum Literary Press
15850 N Thompson Peak Pkwy, 2176
Scottsdale, AZ 85260

solumpress.com

PAPERBACK ISBN 979-8-9898558-6-5
EBOOK ISBN 979-8-9898558-7-2

Cover art and design by Nastia Sarah Christolini and Nastia Bychkova. Concept based on *Lady Justice* as depicted by iStock.com/travelview.
Interior design by Riley Bounds and Sarah Christolini.
Author photo by Melissa Daughters, MKDaughters Photography. Used with permission.

LIBRARY OF CONGRESS CATALOGUING-IN-PUBLICATION DATA
Name: McCoy, Emma, author.
Title: This voice has an echo / emma mccoy
Description: Scottsdale, AZ: Solum Literary Press, 2024.
Identifiers: LCCN 2024942691
ISBN: 979-8-9898558-6-5 (print)
ISBN 979-8-9898558-7-2 (ePub)
Subjects: BISAC: POETRY / General / Subjects & Themes - Religious / American - General / Women Authors
LC record available at https://lccn.loc.gov/2024942691

to my father, for everything

      and to my council of poetic women: Katie, Bettina,
        and Margarita

CONTENTS

LISTENING

RENEWAL

Acknowledgments and Gratitude

Special thanks to the following journals for publishing poems found in this collection:

Amethyst Review ("'Israel's Hands,' by Unknown")

The Chimes ("unstoppable force, meet immovable object" and "drawn into water")

Clayjar Review ("Some of the oldest poetry in the Bible")

Earth and Altar ("Washing women as recipients of prophecy")

Ekstasis Magazine ("Elijah assures Adam and Eve that they will leave hell soon")

Foreshadow Magazine ("A voice in the darkness")

Heart of Flesh Literary Journal ("Fruit trees for the fearful")

Unconventional Courier ("Seriously dangerous religion" and "Dinner Party, With a Ouija Board")

    This book was borne from something I obsessed over during the worst of the pandemic: what is it like to hear God speak? I found God speaks through a whisper, a feeling, a burning bush, a shouting voice, as water in the desert. This desire to encounter the God of prophecy led me to the Old Testament and all the prophets He used to lead and discipline Israel. As I began researching and writing, I heard God through the Scripture, the stories, and the love of everyone around me who helped me along the way.

    I want to first thank Katie Manning, Bettina Pedersen, and Margarita Pintado-Burgos for supporting me throughout this project. Thank you for being with me, hearing my pitches, reading my poems, and giving me feedback. Katie, you've read all these poems since I first started three years ago. Thanks for believing in me.

    I also want to thank my friends for listening to me talk about this nonstop for months. Y'all are the best. A special thank-you to

Iain Provan and Mira Balberg for their generous help with my research and perspective on prophecy.

And lastly, thank you, Dad. For raising me in Christ, loving Mom, and wrestling through the Bible with me. I love our translation talks, picking apart cultural connotations, and trying to figure out a way forward. My walk has been long and slow, and yet you've walked it with me. This book is for you. I love you.

THIS VOICE HAS AN ECHO

EXILE

Do not weep for the dead or mourn for him,
But weep continually for the one who goes away;
For he will never return
Or see his native land.

—Jeremiah 22:10

Patience and darkness

What did Jonah say
when he spent three days in darkness?
Did he speak in the hollow space
and ask it to say something back?
Did he prise God from under his fingernails
and weep, because he was running and looking
with equal effort, ending up
in the stomach of the ocean?
Was God in the darkness, damp and bleeding?

Picture Jonah putting Scripture to melody,
humming to keep himself from going mad
as he turned God's prophecy over and under
his tongue, over and under
without swallowing.

A prophet never folds
after "Judas 'scariot Blues" *by Band of Heathens*

In the hours of the early morning
all have left but them,
hazy figures in the smoky room
playing for everything they have to lose.

She doesn't have a face—
just swirling blankness
like the check she signed to get in:
"Isaiah's wife."
His face is purple, the necklace of rope
tossed carelessly over his shoulder.

The dealer never comments,
just pours red wine the woman doesn't touch
and the man sips carefully, carefully.

There are two things up for grabs
on this last hand:
thirty silver coins and a blank check
cashed somewhere known to her.

The man knocks once.
The woman raises another prophecy.
The man is all-in. "You'll go broke, playing like that," she says,
but the man doesn't listen. She shrugs
as the dealer divides the pot and rolls
the last card. She sighs, smoke pouring
from somewhere, and flips her cards.

2

The man rasps, "Looks like you've
been dealt a higher hand than me."
She gets up, silver untouched.
"Well, Judas, at least you have a name."

What Aaron Was Thinking Right Before He Hoisted the Golden Calf Up On The Platform

Like wildfire

The camera tells the story: charred tree trunks
like charcoal sticks, ash clogging the wind,
hot-plate ground cracked and melting.
Camera pans: skeletal houses, warped cars,
a glob of red plastic of the sidewalk
as if a candle were spilled where the four-square
ball rests, out of shape, forever waiting to play.
Helicopter shots: island-high, rows and rows
of husks in grid formation—bone-white,
hulking, dry as tombs and dotted as leprosy
on the edge of the city. The camera tells it.
Sequence cut: the news anchor in polished
blue polyester introduces a politician,
an expert, a firefighter, a New York lawyer
whose resort shares dropped. Then, in crisp, detached
tone, "Please welcome Haggai, a local community
leader, who would like to say a few words of hope
for all the tourist businesses and people
who lost their vacation homes in this devastating
destruction." Camera shifts: a dark-eyed man
in front of a charcoal house, a young girl
behind him, holding a terrified dog.
For a moment, there's only the wind. Ash
thick as breathing. Behind the camera,
the need for platitude before breakfast.
The man speaks to the lens: "You drink
of this land and are never satisfied. You
think to build a house on the bones
of the dead. The money will fall
from hand to pocket to floor."
The camera cuts.
Commercial break.

Ezekiel and the Exile

I

I am made a watchman
for Israel, the spark
that watches the hammer
against the anvil
and calls from above
"Stop! Leave the hot
hell-ground!" yet brittle
metal still breaks
and falls among the coals.

II

Mourn with me Israel,
for God has shown me
the mysteries. Your slander
will become your gravestone;
even the mountains
will turn away. Your altars
will ensnare you and pick
your bones like carrion.
Violence has grown up
into a rod of wickedness.
None shall remain.

III

I carry my baggage on my back
and walk, like those with no home
are forced to do.

IV

For the sake
of His name God
came down hard!
A rock in an anthill—
we go scurrying
across the desert
so that God can tell
the nations that *this*
is why we keep His
name holy. This is
a lamentation and has
become a lamentation.

V

I lose my wife
and still I speak,
for God too has lost
his bride.

VI

The watchman has
a lonely job; I should know,
nerves frayed
at the edges.
Poised on a hair trigger
to shout
when the hammer falls.
The wicked often
hear the warning;
the righteous can't feel
hot hell-ground beneath
their feet and splinter
against the anvil.

VII

I am knee-deep
in a valley of dry bones,
sun bleached bones,
no breath in them.
Such is a nation
of altars and idols
who will not see
the river flowing
from the temple.
Thus says the LORD God:
I gave my people
to the nations
according to their
iniquity, and the
nations have seen
My judgement.

Even Whole Foods Isn't Beyond the Reach of God

He was in the line at Whole Foods when she approached him, and he didn't recognize her, not at first. Then he crossed his arms, couldn't keep the petulance out of his voice. "It's too much, they're just too much, and don't deserve a second chance like that." She gave a hmmmm, and he saw it: God was wearing a floral-print sundress. "You know," she said, "I love them too." Jonah looked at the twelve-dollar brie in his hand and sighed. "I really hate it here." She slid him a twenty and chuckled. "You'll need your energy. We've a long way to go."

From Habbakuk's subpoenaed text messages

1/4/08
2:13 PM
The verdict was today. No more chances for appeals.
1/4/08
2:15 PM
I just keep wondering what's the point to all this. If these corrupt courts will ever change. If anyone is listening.
1/4/08
2:15 PM
No, I know you are.

1/5/08
10:12 AM
Why can't someone guilty be found guilty? Why can't there be consequences when he drinks too much?
1/5/08
10:13 AM
Consequences later is not the same thing as consequences now.

1/8/08
7:45 PM
I just . . . I found out he bribed the judge. I have proof, but I was shown out of the courthouse. What am I doing? What is anyone doing? What are you doing?
1/8/08
7:47 PM
It'd be faster if I just did this whole thing myself.

1/20/08
6:03 AM
Hey.

1/20/08
6:03 AM
Please tell me it'll be all right in the end. Please tell me you're listening. Please tell me I won't always feel this alone.

1/20/08
6:05 AM
[Deleted message]

[This court has decided the defendant has incited violence against this court, and will be punished to the fullest extent of the law.]

Washing women as recipients of prophecy

Malachiyahu comes back to the launderers
who gather their boiling vats around the ruins
of the city. "He's back!" the women cry.
Their sleeves are rolled up past the elbows,
dresses knotted at the knees as they sweat
and stir and sweat and stir. Malachiyahu
chuckles and pulls back his hair, starts
slicing soap bars so thick it comes off
in flakes the size of Passover bread.
"What news today?" he asks.
"The temple has been finished!" one says.
"My sister has finally made it back with her family,"
says another. "No word from my father,"
sighs another. It takes decades to leave Babylon behind.
Decades more to stir and sweat
over earth that was salted behind you.
"What news from Adonai?" the women ask.
Malachiyahu holds up a stained shirt.
He drags the tough soap across it.
"Like a launderer's soap, God will cleanse
you. Like the mortar beneath you,
God will build you. Like the sun
above you, God will blister and peel you
and stir you in vats until you emerge
spitting soap and can stand on your own."
The fatherless woman, the one with no words
to spare, flushed with heat hums and clicks
her tongue. "Sounds like a love story to me."
She does not defend her words, doesn't need to.
The women know what she means.

Moses, Between the Before and After
Lopez Island, Washington

The tide recedes, reveals, reinvents the strip
of sandy ground. Not quite enough to cross
the next island. I am used to waiting.
The sand is cold, coarse, calculating
how long it has until the tide returns.
I am used to the movement of water.
The promised land is somewhere,
but the tide has not sprung it forth.
I do not know how I got here. For how long.
I am good at waiting.

I know I can never go home.

The plans for you

Open-mic night at the drop-in center
is always interesting, especially in winter.
For people with nowhere else to go,
the linoleum floor is its own country. Stained walls
the overlooked cousin to stained glass, sticky
smell of lemon cleaner and smoke baked
into the blankets. Flyers on the wall advertise
clean-and-sober programs, EBT, yoga, financial
literacy classes, and a moving service that just says
Call Dave with an incomplete phone number.
Open-mic is just starting. A dog in a bright pink harness
shivers. A pile of coats with a tentative hand sticking
out is told to stop smoking indoors. A woman drinks
sickly-sweet instant apple cider. Up front,
a man is incoherent in the microphone—feedback
whines like the speaker has a mouth. The man
sits down. A tentative fight breaks out, is broken
up by staff, and no one so much as looks. Favorite
pallets on the floor are already claimed, in themselves
a country, an untouchable place. Someone won't stop
singing. From the microphone, a ten-minute reading
from the script of *It's a Wonderful Life* that proves
unpopular. More popular, a rant about the donated
bagels from this morning that were moldy. Most
popular, a breathtaking woman, teeth ravaged,
complaining about the new law against loitering.
In the middle of the broken poems
and I-hate-the-courts speeches and teary pleas
for family—and for one woman, silent swaying
for three minutes—the *chunking* of the stapler
draws attention. "You want to say something,
Jeremiah?" a huge, hulking man near the front says.
Jeremiah, slight and wild-eyed, picks up the papers

14

he's been stapling obsessively and shuffles them.
"You've been dying to talk so damn bad," someone
else says. "They keep kicking you out of the churches
and shit—just get up there and get it over with."
Discussion ensues. Staff break this up too.
Silent, Jeremiah walks to the front, passing the papers
along as he goes. Sitting cross-legged, everyone
without a home has to lean in to hear. Most don't.
"Everything will be all right," he says. "God's in control,
especially when you aren't. He knows where you're going
and where you've been, and you'll have everything
you need." A handful of people scoff. Some are already
asleep. Others look at him with something like hope.
The papers fall to the ground, forgotten. Just as they
were torn from the light poles and the sidewalks
and the subway walls and the corkboards in trendy
coffee shops. They read, staples at odd angles:
Everyone in this city will die. Even you.
The papers will be tossed tomorrow, a staff member
grumbling about removing staples for recycling.
But tonight, open-mic concludes with staticky silence
and terse instructions to turn down and shut off the lights.
Outside, snow splats against the street, wet and heavy.

DEATH

i hope death is like being carried to your bedroom when
you were a child & fell asleep on the couch during a
family party. i hope you can hear the laughter from the
next room.
—lilies abandoned, or X

When Job's three friends heard all about the troubles that had come
upon him, they set out from their homes . . . when they saw him
from a distance, they could hardly recognize him; they began to weep
aloud, and they tore their robes and sprinkled dust on their heads.
Then they sat on the ground with him for seven days and seven
nights. No one said a word.
—Job 2:11–13

Dinner Party, With A Ouija Board

He watches the board shift
on the coffee table

to the delighted coos
of the brightly dressed women

and the disguised gasps
of the richly suited men.

Smoke lingers in the air
as they ask will there be war?

The papers say no,
the president says no,

and in the clink of slim bracelets
and candy-colored nails

the board says no too.
He catches the eye of a woman

slinking toward the exit
amid the silky cheers of guests

with the beginnings of worry

on her smoky eyelids

and raises his glass sardonically.

Amos

The announcer shifts on the temple steps, unrolls a scroll, bellows to the restless crowd: "Here comes Amos, first of the writing prophets! Today he addresses the nation—a Word for us all from Adonai, God Most High." A few snickers puncture the silence, but most just watch as Amos climbs the steps, hammers a single sheet of parchment to the temple doors with brutal efficiency. He throws the hammer to the ground and it cracks like a death knoll.

Prepare to meet your God

Amos returns to his vineyards to drink wine and wait.

Ehud Holds Court at the Bar

No, seriously, this really happened.
Listen, listen—tell those guys
back there to shut up. Never mind,
they're too drunk to listen.

Anyway, y'all know how I'm left-handed right?
I hid my sword—
What? Yes, I carried it with me everywhere.
Yes, like a cell phone, I guess.
But I hid it on my right leg so those stupid guards
never thought I had a blade on me.
And King Eglon, that stupid, sweaty idiot
thought I had a prophecy for him.
Well, I did say I had a secret *deber*, but the *deber*
was my sword, buried to the hilt. Even
my hand disappeared in all the fat!
I twisted, he squealed, I couldn't even find
bone to grate my sword against.
You're gonna doubt me? Have you ever picked
intestines from under your fingernails?
Then he shit himself, all over
the floor so the servants thought he locked
himself in the bathroom. By the time they broke
the door down—well, you know the rest.
You don't? Haven't you ever read the Bible?
Yeah, that's how it happened. Were you there?
Didn't think so. Anyway, the land knew peace
for eighty fuckin' years. Older than you!

Next round's on me, who can top that?

Elijah assures Adam and Eve that they will leave hell soon

(apocalypse, verb. Greek, apokálypsis, meaning "unveiling" or "uncovering")

Though "soon" is a word that has no real meaning.
He is in between heaven and earth on the fast track
past death when he sees them and takes a moment to rest.

Ascension is heavy work. The first mother to ever lose a child
wants to know if anyone buried her baby's shoes. The first father
to ever lose a child asks after Elisha, How do you think he'll do?

Elijah only has a moment, but he says it anyway. Eve laughs
like Sarai and Adam reminds him they died but a breath ago.
If anything, a prophet should know that the ages collapse

into each other like parchment layers melting between heaven
and earth. And tucked away, waiting for nothing longer than a
        breath,
is the apocalypse of buried baby shoes.

drawn out of water

I

fire.
  "here I am"
the ground you stand on
is holy, I am the God
of your father's father, I will be
with you always. row go! I have commanded.
strike the dust of the ground, there is no
one like the LORD, worship me!
I AM WHO I AM.
plague, darkness,
blood.

II

wailing.
      bread without yeast.
           Passover, passed over
               and so they plundered proud egypt.
                   carry bones down the red sea road,
did God
                     bring them to the desert
to die in a mass grave?
               night brings hope, drive the sea
back, divided.
          feet on dry ground, remembering
       "the LORD will fight for you"
    working wonders,
faithful.

23

III

bread.
   "what is it?"
the LORD provided.
come before the LORD, he has
heard your grumbling, take what need dictates.
wafer with honey, white like coriander,
and yet they put the LORD to the test.
leftovers full of maggots,
still unsatisfied.
moses cried.
sand.

IV

sinai.
      do not approach.
like smoke from a furnace
      the mountain trembled violently.
tell the israelites: I am the LORD
      your God and there is no other. you shall, shall not.
do not harm the widow, the fatherless,
      I will certainly hear their cry.
forty days, forty nights
      moses listens.
promise.

Face it forward
The first of Joel's sonnets

Who here has read the sacred scrolls and books?
Which one among you knows the history,
forgoes pride, hypocrisy, haughty looks
because they know full well the misery
ahead? Look to the past, see the future
wearing its familiar skin, you blink
and it's past you already—no truer
thing, the slow march of end to end. You think
you're ready for justice? It comes thief-like
when you're weak and whiny, complaining you
didn't have enough time. God will streamline
the coming thunderstorm, out-raining you
each time. Tear your hearts before tearing clothes,
when the rain stops only God ever knows.

Obadiah informs Edom they're guilty

of accessory to murder

Crows picking
at the corpse
of Israel
do not escape
God's net

The prophet's midwife

Puah, did you know?
That there would be a baby boy
meant to save your whole world,
cuddled deep in courage
at the bottom of a wicker basket.

Oh the midwife had a knife,
cut the cord and lied to save a life.

Puah, did you know?
That God caressed your steel-lined spine
when you answered the tyrant
in his living room and placed
the women of your world behind you.

Oh the midwife had a knife,
cut the cord and lied to save a life.

Puah, did you know?
That written in lines beyond your lifetime
were the riverbanked beginnings
of freedom, born of blood and muffled
screams and the courage to lie.

Oh the midwife had a knife,
cut the cord and lied to save a life.

Puah, did you know?
That there were silent searing looks,
linking river rushes and losing a battle
against the dark; women sealing hope
in baskets and birthing-room deceptions.

Oh the midwife had a knife,
cut the cord and lied to save a life.

Puah, you must've known
the danger, might've felt that under
the whip and the dust and the night labors
were the stirrings of prophecy,
born under a lie, and sealed with hope.

Oh the midwife had a knife,
cut the cord and lied and saved a life.

Elijah's hit single, "Showdown"
Throwing the gauntlet, old-school

I'm a thunderbolt in desert clothing
drinking water from the river, ravens
bring my food. My enemies stay loathing
me, hating on me in my God haven.
Eight hundred lying prophets, come to me!
Let's climb a mountain and battle it out
over flame; Israel can come and see
your bullshit. I'll laugh and rattle it out
of you! What, is your god taking a shit
somewhere? Your straw man god can't save you now,
I'll swing my godly butcher's sword and slit
your throats up to chins and lips and eyebrows.
Streams run red with the blood of lying men.
You wanna fight God? The truth? Try me, then.

Liminal

"The words of Jeremiah end here."

He knew.
Prophets get to see death coming.

He witnessed it all and refused
to speak of it—
the gnawing hunger, alive and angry.
The shattered pottery, bedsheets
burned in the street, a hand curling
under a crushing stone.

He knew.
Prophets know the smell of death.

The festering sores under iron bands,
the stench of rotting flesh
and piss and vomit and blood.
Most haunting: a young boy,
spread-eagle in a doorway with his throat
cut in a gaping smile.

He knew.
Prophets don't get to retire.

When he lay bleeding on Egyptian sand
with dented skull, broken ribs, numb mouth,

he struggled to breathe. He knew.

Couldn't conjure up
regret.

THE TALMUD MAKES AN INTERJECTION

for the conversations
of the learned were written
and this they had to say:

The Gemara asks with regard to the prophetesses
recorded in the *baraita*: Who were the seven prophetesses?
The Gemara answers:
Sarah, Miriam, Deborah, Hannah, Abigail, Huldah, and Esther.
—Talmud Bavli, Megillah 14a

God of Sarah

When God came to me inside the tent I was kneading
bread; my husband was outside with the men
and they promised us a living future
and heard me laugh at God (why did you laugh, Sarah?).

My husband was outside with the men, hearing
dust shift in the heat of the day,
but when God heard me laugh (I didn't laugh, Lord)
God knew the surprise and sorrow there.

The dust shifted outside, uncomfortable,
because what God hands out miracles like rainstorms?
But God heard the surprise and sorrow
in a laugh, knew the loneliness of woman.

Does God hand out miracles like rainstorms?
My faith is thin as pepper flakes, as thin
as a husband who does not know the loneliness of woman.
That day God promised I would be a mother

though my faith was thin as pepper flakes.
When God came to me inside the tent I was needing
a miracle; God promised I would be a mother
and go, laughing, into the future.

drawn into water

I remember the sand under my feet
when I watched my brother on the river—
caught in the reeds, a prophecy in a wicker basket.
There came Pharaoh's daughter. I was afraid

but watched my brother on the river,
God whispering mystery in my ear.
I, so afraid, saw Pharaoh's daughter coming.
She sent me back to Mother.

God whispered mystery in my ear,
always overflowing into song and tragedy
and sending me back to Mother.
My brother grew old in exile.

He will overflow into song and tragedy
like the guttural sound of freedom.
My brother grew old in exile
and we led an exodus across the sea

to the guttural sound of freedom.
God is in the air we breathe, He told me.
We led an exodus across the sea
and felt the heat of the desert.

God is in the air we breathe. He told me
to keep His commandments and love without restraint.
I feel the heat of the desert,

the cool uncertainty of an ocean split apart.

Keep His commandments. Love without restraint.
I sing the victory song as a vision for the future amid
the cool uncertainty of an ocean split apart.
The salt tangles my hair and closes my eyes.

The victory song is a vision for the future
and I remember the sand under my feet.
The salt tangles my hair and closes my eyes. I am
caught in the reeds—a prophecy in a wicker basket.

unstoppable force, meet immovable object
a sonnet of Deborah

I'm a God-given mouthpiece: a prophet.
They call me a judge; I can do that too,
watch the war-hungry men who would profit
from God's wisdom, falter, in my newsroom.
I was shocked—call me a maybe-quitter.
When he came in, brawn-bared, and asked for me
I thought what, you need a babysitter?
God has not hidden me, my mysteries.
He lays them all in lines like graveyard rows
and so I see from the hills, in visions,
a woman with a bloody stake who knows
a ground-teeth promise and God's precision.
Human pride and fear tend to intermix.
I don't care for your death-bound politics.

A time for joy

On weekends, Hannah braids
her son's hair down his back
long and thick.

She doesn't mind the visitation
rights with God,
not when she gets to know
her son lives in the same world,
breathes the same air as her.

Hannah braids, and remembers
the feel of the temple steps
when she prayed desperately.

God remembers that when she prayed,
she prayed not for her torment
at the hands of Peninnah to end.

As she braids, her sleeves
slip down showing shiny burns,
little scars a decade old.
She doesn't show her son,
his back to her. She doesn't show
her husband because he does not
deserve her pain.

She only shows God
on visitation weekends,

air caressing her forearms
as she braids and braids and braids.

Abigail
(her name is the whole title, remember it)

Oh, by all the tribes, I'm going to kill him.
I'm wearing my house shoes, damn.
I hope they're preparing the food.
Why did my father marry me to him?
Adonai, give me words, give me words.
There's a rock in my shoe, damn.
I can see the army from over here.
I can fix this, I can do all things,
I am someone with a face and words.
Why did I change my dress but not my shoes?
Why did he say the things he did?
It is not my day to die.
Adonai, make it not my day to die.
My husband is probably drunk by now. Damn.
I have to do EVERYTHING around here.
Oh, the army is so close. There's David.
They won't kill me on sight
(the one good time to be a woman).
The rock is out of my shoe.
They're coming up to me.

Here are my words.
Here are my words.

Consultation, Part 1

In which President Josiah sends an intern to the offices of Zeldman &
Wright

The secretary directed me to Huldah's office
with a grim *good luck*. I clutched the portfolio

to my chest and skittered down the hall. Cardboard
cubicles and mahogany walls and fresh-grad lawyers

answering phones and tearing legal-yellow paper
off in sheets. Mints on a desk. Spit-shined shoes.

I let the details push me along. At the brass *Wright*
nameplate I stopped and watched her at the desk.

Plum-wine suit, beige nails, and coiffed hair in waves.
She held the phone like it'd done her wrong. "You know,"

she said, city accent somehow sounding rich, "I doubt
you'd say that to me if I were a man. The law doesn't

change just because you want it to." I looked down
the hall. Each seat held a young man, coiffed and serious.

In the office, the skyline spread behind Huldah like
a mosaic. Broken. Whole. "If you want to ask Zeldman

and get billed twice, be my guest." She hung up with
a click, like teeth clacking against a shut mouth.

I dropped the portfolio and papers flooded the carpet.
I picked them up and left. I had forgotten my question.

Somehow, it didn't matter.

Miss Universe has a conversation with Death in the waiting room

How long have
you been here?

> A while
> This is usually a good spot
> to wait
> Saves me a lot of time

How do you mean?

> Oh, it's a safe bet
> I'll be needed at least once
> every few days
> If I wait here I don't
> have to walk as far

Makes sense to me.
I have often heard death
described as a journey.

> You're quite calm, you know

Well.
I decided to be here.
I know the consequences.

42

                                                    Most don't
                                        Are you sure it's worth it?

What an odd question
from you. Yes,
there's a whole universe
of people who need me
and I've had a long time
to be prepared.

Are you here
because my name won't
be called?

                                                    I don't know yet
                                                    I'm playing the odds
                                        though I have a feeling I'll lose
                                                            this time

Really?

                                                            We'll see

I suppose so.

I like your jacket.
It looks like the night sky.

Thank you
A carpenter made it
for me, oh, about
five hundred years from now

Your crown is beautiful

Thank you.
The weight is enough
to kill someone.

Perhaps

I do believe that's
your name being called

That it is.
Thank you, Death, for waiting.

May we meet again
not so soonly

Congratulations,
Esther

A qualification to the Talmud's interjection
an email from an expert

RE: Happy retirement! Question about the OT as well
From: Iain Provan
To: Emma McCoy

Hi Emma!
The Talmud: it has considerable authority for Jews, but no intrinsic authority for Christians. So it's interesting to read in order to get some Jewish perspectives, but we need to compare it to Scripture and assess it on that basis. Sometimes it is going to help us, and sometimes not. I'll be interested to hear what a rabbi has to say about the list of prophets—how he explains all the names on the list.
Best wishes from Scotland—we are about to go hiking in Ireland, so we won't have computers there.
Iain Provan

not sent from My iPhone

An addendum to the Talmud's interjection
lines from an email from Mira Balberg, professor of Judaic Studies at UCSD

The Talmud is inventive, creative / uninterested in a "real meaning"
/ The rabbis read prophecy as God speaking / yes / but also as divine
revelation / Anyone in contact with a "holy spirit" / even in passing
counts / Miriam, Huldah, Deborah have the benefit of the text /
Sarah, Hannah, Abigail, Ester / they were described as very beautiful
/ the old religious men conclude / the beauty is actually a holy spirit
/ The Talmud is its own fantastic and wondrous beast

LISTENING

It must be that when God speaketh, he should communicate not one thing, but all things: should fill the world with his voice; should scatter forth light, nature, time, souls from the centre of the present thought . . . whenever a mind is simple, and receives a divine wisdom, then old things pass away . . . all things are made sacred by relation to it,—one thing as much as another.
—Ralph Waldo Emerson

In the undertow

I watch the rain through a honey-colored window. It's still early and dark. My damp hair curls and frizzes on the edges. My coffee is warm. It's bitter without sugar. I shift in my seat. Low conversation fills the shop. I check the boxes in my head and push my pencil around the table. I sigh, a low buzz in my veins. For the third time, the newspaper catches my eye. It smells like wet paper. Ink bleeding to the edges.
God centered living.
I skip lightly over phrases. Endless death. False world. Contrite and lowly. Promises. I catch the byline. *Isaiah, temple prophet*. I swirl my coffee. It's cold now. Push my pencil some more. Shove unfinished papers in my bag. Zip my coat. I need to pick up diapers. I'm getting to work later and later. Across the street, the homeless shelter starts taking shape in the hesitant daylight. My phone rings. I leave the newspaper behind.

The blood is not on her hands

As sure as time, history is repeating itself, and as sure as man is man,
history is the last place he'll look for his lessons.
—Harper Lee, *Go Set A Watchman*

And when humans flooded the earth
(for they made no rainbow oaths)
the watchman saw, and the watchman heard.

The oceans boiled in the deep and churned
the great cities to a watery close.
And when humans flooded the earth

they scrambled on steel boats, chose berths
ranked by wealth and color and who knows
what else. The watchman saw, and heard

from her lighthouse on the mountains. Birds
brought her news of where they chose
to go after the humans flooded the earth.

She tried her best, for what it's worth,
to warn the ships that got too close
to the rocky shores. The watchman saw, heard

the scraping and grinding, the curdling
screams of shipwreck. She supposed
that when humans flooded the earth,
she was the only one who saw, and heard.

49

Zechariah's Niner Niners

In the two thousandth twenty second
year, the word of God came to Zecha.
"I will bless this land, and there will
be freedom in the streets once again."
Zecha had the barest memories
of his freedom—children in the street
and no memory of the elderly
ones perched on fronted porches, watching
life go by. He prayed, *God end the war.*

It is written: "Ask the LORD for rain
in the springtime, it is the LORD who
sends the thunderstorms." Zecha didn't
know what rain felt like; he knew the bombs
falling from the sky to raze the earth.
He knew some other government sent
them, knew his land's been dry and cracked, been
pot-holed and blood-soaked and torn to bits,
been scattered. He prayed, *God end the war.*

In the two thousandth twenty second
year, the word of God came to Zecha.
He was barefoot in a bare backyard
when he saw a dry, sinful basket—
a wicked, grinning, sitting woman.
An angel shoved her in the basket
and took it far away. Zecha wept.
The years of war, coming to a close.
Zecha began preparing the streets.

Nathan's College Haikus

1.

We're all having fun
when Nathan just ruins it
again. C'mon, man.

No one cares that she
tore her roommate's favorite dress
and lied about it.

Tonight's her birthday
and you're gonna bring it up?
We're having dinner.

So what if she has
plenty of dresses, who cares?
You can't un-tear it.

Please just sit back down
and don't make a scene again.
I won't say it twice.

2.

Think of it like this:
they're all eating college food
off slimy steel plates

which is gross at best
and then Nathan tells the truth.
Which is gross at best.

To students, at least.
And others, because who wants
to be reflected?

Anyway, truth slides
off them like slime and sticks no
where. No one's surprised.

3.

Ugh, god, he's the friend
who doesn't know when to stop.
Why can't he just quit?

I got the job fair
and square, and he tells me this
fucking weird story

about a rich man
and sheep. Sure, I had other
offers, but who cares?

She should have worked more
if she wanted to get it,
known the right people.

I am not to blame.
Why can't he just let it go?
No one's listening.

A voice in the darkness
Samuel and his visions

Listen! Here, in the dark,
someone calling your name.
Not the old prophet, sleeping
heavy, nor his sons who
sleep dreamless every night.
Look! There, on the inner steps
of the temple, a woman praying
and pleading with God.
Her whispers float over cold
marble and you shift
your child's feet. Familiar?
Perhaps, like a dream
that comes once a year.
You blink once and she's gone,
quiet like the name
just outside your reach.
Wait! Someone else must be here
in shadowed corridors and empty
nighttime splendor
for you can feel it
as close as your next breath.

Now, in those days there
were no frequent visions

but the dark seems less scary
and you can see the faith
the future holds, with oil
and pride and pastures.
This must be what your mother

prayed over you when she
dropped you off on the temple
steps, blessing personified.
You, child, are love embodied,
proof of a warm and living God
who spins dreams. You see
His mysteries this night, and every night,
walking past prophets and sons,
feet cold on marble, head
light and full of promise.
Breathe, Kingmaker, and
fall asleep to the sound of
your name whispered with love.

Say it again: sons and daughters
The second of Joel's sonnets

And Joel wrote on the subway walls: "After
shame has died three times over, the Spirit
will pour out of the cracks like new laughter
and every single child will feel it."
Sons and daughters, sons and daughters, scholars
draw territory lines and camp out there
to uplift the prophetess or maul her.
They all split hairs but no one asks how dare
we carve a prophecy that's hard to see,
meant for daughters, gifted spray paint on brick
or concrete. And when the prophecies
run out of the cracks in the walls, they slip
past the scholars and drop into the hands
of daughters and sons, according to plan.

Seriously dangerous religion
for Iain Provan, upon his retirement

When he was studying theology, my dad inadvertently
showed me how to befriend a professor:
build him a deck while your children eat pancakes
inside. Take delight in his wit, in the accent so thick
you'd need a crowbar to stir it.
Go fishing, read his book, graduate
and wait as he watches your children graduate in turn.

I have many memories of him but my favorite is this:
we are snowed in, all of us. We go to the bottom
of our steep hill to assess that tricky turn,
to see if he can make his flight, or stay another night.
There are already two cars in the ditch,
writing etched in snow and swerving tire treads
showing black against the white.
He is a prophet of the old ages, watching that third
car pull slowly forward I often wonder what the driver
was thinking—seeing the old man with the eyes of God
shake his head and point at the writing on the road,
and how he bore witness to a third casualty
of friction and gravity.

You Are That Man

*A thing may happen and be a total lie; another thing may not happen
and be truer than the truth.*
—Tim O'Brien, *The Things They Carried*

I cannot tell the truth as it is.
It would not fit
through the door, its face
cruel and unfamiliar.

The happening-truth
must be stalked cautiously
like a deer in the desert.
To pin it down
and force it through the front door
right into the home,
I must tell story-truth
and hope it is gentle enough
to be heard unguarded,

so that the deer can creep
behind the chair
in all its cruel glory.

The dreamer

Daniel had a dream
    (the spirit of holy gods
    no mystery
    too difficult)

Daniel had a dream of writing
    (the chief of magicians
    call for Daniel
    he will tell me
    what the writing means)

Daniel had a dream of beasts
    (the trampling
    troubling me
    wild wild to come)

Daniel had a dream of seventy sevens
    (captivity lasts seventy years
    why does he tell me?
    Gabriel says do not be afraid
    but I am)

Daniel had a dream of a man
    (he was face down
    I am a man
    and his god is not)

Daniel had a dream of deliverance

(names in the book
a time and half a time
remember me, remember me)

This voice has an echo

Elijah wakes in the night
and his mind
echoes echoes echoes
with the sounds
of soldiers screaming,
the trickles then streams
of blood mixing with dust,
pasting his boots
He hears the desert,
sweats it out, the empty
click of his gun and it
echoes echoes echoes
He fists the sheets,
clenches his tongue
but the walls are an altar
of fire and the heat
crackles his mind how it
echoes echoes echoes
The crust under his nails
won't go away, his pit
of a stomach his swivel
of a neck always snapping
and looking and the glare
of the rifle's body
warm against his cheek
and the dull thud of the bullet
in flesh
echoes echoes echoes
He lays back, exhausted
unsleeping and spent
past the draft
He's safe now,
isn't he? He is awake in the night

on damp sheets in burnt walls
and fried eyes and he is tired
When he whispers,
I want to die it
echoes echoes echoes
and God hears it

And if God doesn't hear,
then He'll hear
the echo and
the echo and
the echo

RENEWAL

"I will repay you for the years the
locusts have eaten . . .
You will have plenty to eat, until
you are full,
and you will praise the
name of the Lord your
God,
who has worked wonders for
you;
never again will my people be
shamed."
—Joel 2:25-26

The river is not divided
Miriam's second victory song

Miriam and I are sitting
by the bank of the Blackfoot
in Montana. I throw a rock
across the surface, it sinks.

You'll ruin the fishing
that way.

I know.

Her curly hair is held back
with a yellow bandana. Thick
eyebrows, clinking jewelry,
her hands don't stop moving.

So you're a prophet?

A poet.

Let's call it both.
Can you answer me
this, sing it or tell it,
I don't mind—

Please stop throwing
rocks. We might fish
later.

Sorry.
What do you know
of loneliness?
What does God know
of loneliness?

That's two questions.

64

Can you not
speak for both?

           Miriam thinks on that one.
           We are knee to knee, not
           :n the desert, but outside
           the Promised land. The river
           flows, but it's just water.

                        There are many kinds
                      of loneliness. The scholars
                      debate if Moses and Aaron
                      are my real brothers. What
                  does it matter? Their love was real.

But you are remembered.

                        I sang a song of victory
                      but I dream of drowning
                      men and horses,
                      the choked screams.
                      I dream of the golden gleam
                      of an idol, the heat
                      of fear and anger.

What hurts?
What is weighted?

                        My chest.
                      My hands.
                      I fear I will wander forever,
                      and God will go silent.

           The river gurgles.
           She has closed her eyes
           and gone still, even the wind
           dares not tangle her curls.

In the beginning . . .

                            In the beginning
                                  God created.
                     There was only God,
          and God filled the universe.

Was it because
God was lonely?

                          All I know is God
                       created, created a
                         Beginning
                 and filled it with life.

            She grabs my hand.
              Am I broken?

                     It is not good for us
                         to be alone.
               I sang a victory song,
        and did not sing it alone.
            My nightmares wake
                   my brothers,
       and we battle the night
                   together.

          Miriam takes her bag,
     pulls out bread crusty and salted
            and breaks it.

                                 Just ask.

The river rushes for a moment,
the flood of water audible.
She flinches, hands a piece
of bread to me.

"Israel's Hands" by Unknown

It was nearing springtime when Ezekiel visited his sister
in the city and brought his sprawling notebooks.
She was almost done with an exhibit—her living room
on the fifteenth floor covered with canvas and paint,
the concrete floor splattered and everywhere, everywhere
was God. "Tell it to me again," she said, and stood in front
of the biggest canvas of them all. Ezekiel turned a page.
"Think of it like this, my-people-who-will-not-listen.
You are walking, passing by a field. In the ditch to the left
you hear wailing. A baby! Still slippery with blood and warm,
like a calf born in the dirt, kicking and screaming with fear.
You pick it up, wipe away the grime with your jacket—"
The painting is taking shape. She's feathered the background
softly, green fading into blue, the cool mud of a resting field
clumping at the front. The way her prophet brother tells it,
the baby is afraid, but there! off to the left, a speck of red,
a tiny fist waving above the grass, a hint of a leg kicking
in defiance. "You know, in the moment, everything. How
that child will grow to hate you, curse you, throw your love
in the dirt. And still you wrap it, and take it with you."
She flicks her wrist, and there, in the corner:
a pair of hands reaching to meet the bloody fist.

Gomer never wanted a picket fence

and spent her nights crawling the streets
for the edge in her blood and Hosea had waited
and at some point, it just wasn't worth it anymore.
She had torn up her aprons and forgot the children
at school, gone days without coming home and let
the yard run wild. She never wanted it, not at all.
She doesn't know when it happened, but it did.
She scheduled interviews and never went,
took grocery money to parties and spat when Hosea
asked where she was going. She knew
she was married off as an example, it was part
of his prophecy thing. Once a whore,
always a whore. But it became so exhausting,
and there was something that didn't add up.
Maybe it was the third child, the one that finally
looked like him, resting on her hip while she waited
for the other two to come home on the bus.
Maybe it was the way he never yelled, not once
in years, waited up for her every night, washed
the blood from her hair when she was beaten
by that guy on 4th Street. It felt like kicking
a puppy, honestly, even when she was the one kicked.
Maybe it was the way he calmly pushed away
the snide soccer moms and their slimy husbands
with the wandering hands. Never fighting, just walking
away, like he actually meant what he said.
At some point, it was easier to spend the night in
and maybe, just maybe, when the bruises had faded
and he was still in the living room, this whole God thing
had something to it.

Hosea always wanted a love story

and God gave him
one like His own

Waiting
with the light on

Faithful
and bruising

Offering

I have heard God speak
under the milk-spray sky,
stars dripping to earth,
a break in desert loneliness.
I have heard God promise
in the form of strangers
in my tent, tearing bread
and dipping it in oil.
I have heard God laugh
like my wife, wrapping
a sticky baby in cloth,
a future curled in tiny hands.

God speaks. This I know
like how I know my tents
are temporary and my wealth
won't save me. I have heard
God speak in the night,
like a priest, from a rock,
in a lamb's mouth, through
my wife, from down a well,
in between my tears. So unlike
all these gods, how he promises
what I never dared want.

But nothing touched my heart,
ripped me open and stitched
over it, like the sound of Heaven
as I was holding the knife
over my son, his terrified face
killing me, killing me. How
I thought *of course a god would
ask this of me*. How Heaven cleaved

me like an animal by saying this—

Put down the knife. Forever.

In a Valley of Bones

I am told Ezekiel had a vision
of dry bones, breathless bones,
littering the corpse of a river.

Prophecy is not a competition;
in fact, it has a 99% mortality rate.
But was my master Elijah not the 1%?
Did I not receive twice his portion?
I was not a vision.
My bones still had bite to them,
raised the man who rattled them
and brought him,
confused and breathless,
out of the valley.

A psalm of david

My eyelids pull down
like the sides of our tent
but grandmama calls me closer.

She pulls me in her lap
with hands like the desert
and she smells dark
of the spices that linger
on my tongue at night.

Hesed, she whispers,
beloved, let me tell you a story.
I rub my face, head tilted
downward as my mind
goes far far away

to a foreign land, where
I was grandmama, young
and grieving with
sun-scorched thoughts
and a heart for God.

My days there were
a fleeting shadow,
pulling bitter barley from earth
my feet did not know,
I ate in obedient sorrow.

He called me beloved, daughter.
I will be a mother to kings
and he will pick me up
from out of the dust.

Hesed, she murmurs,
you will be the greatest
of kings, taking God in your heart
after my bones are scattered
at the mouth of the grave.

I love the way my grandmama
shapes her words,
how she makes sweet bread
at sunrise while I watch
the sheep. Tomorrow

feels like a story for later,
so I snuggle deeper
and dream of caves
and oil and music.

Fruit trees for the fearful
The third of Joel's sonnets

He's the coolest therapist I've had yet.
Shoots straight, no bullshit, no hollow statements
like "Just pray through it" or "You know, I bet
God has a good plan for this." I hate this.
Joel sits us outside today, on the grass,
wordless. He says he learned quiet from Job,
a grieving man. "So you won't go to class."
Joel-man never asks questions. "There's no hope,"
I reply. More quiet. The grieving kind.
"One day," he says, "God will give you the years
the sadness has eaten, both fruit and rind.
You won't know what to do with all the pears
and plums and it'll be better than before."
Not placating, no, but something much more.

Consultation, Part 2
In which the Constitution has been rediscovered

"Do you know what this is?"
        she asked him, slowly.

President Josiah shook
his head.

Outside, the Secret Service
shook their heads, too.

Huldah smiled and slid
the portfolio across
the desk.

"It's billable,"
        she said.

Josiah shook his head
and smiled.

"Hope," she added.
        "Tricky, awful hope."

Some of the oldest poetry in the Bible

An unusual woman sat under an unusual tree dispensing justice
—Robert D. Branson, "Judges: A Commentary"

And it was after the death of Joshua
when Israel went to bed with their idols
and everyone did what was right in her own eyes.

And it was after Sisera came against the people
like a hammer on a tent peg when Israel
cried out, like *za'aq*, "Wake up Deborah! Wake up!"

And it was after I pitched my tent under the palm tree
when the warlords came for counsel and God
whispered to me on the breath of the desert.

And it was much after God's anger grew hot
when I held court in the shade as the last judge
of deliverance—did not Sisera perish

and bleed from his brain because Jael came against
him with a hammer and a tent peg? Most blessed
among women, always welcome in my war-room.

And it was much, much later when I was dozing
under my palm tree where I heard the stirrings
of Israel's sin, and the clash of Babylon's shields.

I was startled from my sleep when a girl came
to me in the darkness and asked for God's voice.
With the promise of repentance and exile

in my ears, I sent her away with instructions
to wait in the night and listen for an echo.

A prophecy hidden under the tongue.

And the land knew peace for forty years.

Notes

A prophet never folds: There are a few explicitly named female prophets in the Old Testament: Huldah, Deborah, Miriam, and the "nameless" wife of Isaiah; see Isaiah 8:3 (NIV). While listening to "Judas 'Scariot Blues" one day, I was struck by how little space Isaiah's wife gets at the table, and it tickled me to imagine her and Judas in a poker game.

From Habbakuk's subpoenaed text messages: The book of Habbakuk is focused, to a large degree, on justice. In this string of text messages with God, we only get Habbakuk's texts, which rail against a corrupt court system in a "he said, she said" situation. It can be read two ways: either Habbakuk is the injured party, or he's outraged on someone's behalf.

The plans for you: If you've hung out at a drop-in or low-barrier homeless shelter, this poem might feel familiar. Historically speaking, Jeremiah was a backwoods prophet who would've very much been on the outside. He would've been invisible to most of the city, much like our neighbors experiencing homelessness.

Dinner Party, With A Ouija Board: The Ouija Board is a symbol reminiscent of the condemnation of false prophecy found in Ezekiel 13. I remain intrigued by the one woman at the party who seems to be uncomfortable with everyone saying the same thing.

Amos: Amos was the first of what are considered the writing prophets. He is also the only prophet I've found who got to retire. He was a wealthy man and was allowed to go back to his property after his ministry was finished.

drawn out of water: This poem contains a fixed meter pattern (2, 4, 6, 8, 10, 8, 6, 4, 2, and then alternates odd numbers) and only uses words found in Deuteronomy. Word hunt!

The prophet's midwife: Feel free to hum, "Mary, Did You Know?"

Elijah's hit single, "Showdown": 1 Kings 18:27 contains Elijah's response to the prophets of Ba'al when they were having their showdown on top of the mountain. The insult to Ba'al (who couldn't light the pyre) literally translates from the Hebrew as "relieving himself somewhere." In this sonnet, I've styled Elijah after hip-hop and rap grandstanding, which contrasts nicely against Elijah as a veteran with PTSD in "This voice has an echo." The very event that Elijah was boasting about comes back to haunt him.

THE TALMUD MAKES AN INTERJECTION: The Talmud is a collection of Rabbinic commentary and discussion on Holy texts. This grouping of texts is called the Mishnah, identified by the appearance of the Gemara, which was the group of Jewish scholars having the discussions. There are actually six groups of Gemara total. The Talmud Bavli, which contains the quote on prophetesses, records the Gemara's conclusions, and was published around 500 C.E. by Babylonian scholars. As the Old Testament is a deeply Jewish work of literature, it was crucial for me to include the Talmud's perspective in this book.

A time for joy: The allusion to Peninnah's physical abuse of Hannah is an interpretation of mine. 1 Samuel 1 describes Hannah being "tormented" and I've imagined that to be physical.

Consultation, Part 1: Huldah is one of two explicitly named female prophets from the *Nevi'im*, or what's known as the "prophets" section. Very little is known about her, other than she was the wife of a royal employee, lived in the New Quarter of Jerusalem, and was a respected prophet in her own right.

A qualification to the Talmud's interjection: Iain Provan is a retired professor of Old Testament from Regent College. He's also a family friend who can be fun to track down because he doesn't own a cell phone. Nevertheless, he's a talented scholar, and his wit and genius are on display in his books, which include *Seriously Dangerous Religion* and *Seeking What Is Right: The Old Testament and the Good Life*.

In the undertow: The structure of this poem, like the book of Isaiah, is a chiasm. A chiasm is a literary device, a storytelling structure

81

in a pyramid shape, with one feature of the story acting as the turning point.

Zechariah's Niner Niners: Zechariah has been reimagined in a modern war context. "Niner" is employed to refer to my stanzas of nine lines with nine syllables, as well as how Zecha has been charged with telling Israel they're leaving captivity. The poem contains a verse, verbatim, from Zechariah 10. The woman in the basket is from Zechariah 5.

Nathan's College Haikus: College students don't exactly have the market cornered on being defensive, but it's close.

A voice in the darkness: Another chiasm! Actually, the whole book of Samuel is a chiasm.

Seriously dangerous religion: So I'm about seventeen or so, standing at the bottom of this snowy, icy hill with my father and Iain Provan. There are two cars in the ditch, and this third car, despite being able to see this, decides to take a crack at the hill. I honestly don't know what they were thinking. But maybe that's prophecy.

You Are That Man: Tim O'Brien, you are so awesome.

"Israel's Hands" by Unknown: I wanted to give Ezekiel a sister, a sort of artistic counterpart to his prophetic ministry. She paints a scene from Ezekiel 16.

Gomer never wanted a picket fence: In order to illustrate Israel's unfaithfulness, God commanded the prophet Hosea to marry Gomer, a known prostitute. Gomer's feelings on the matter are never consulted, and I like to think she eventually finds happiness with Hosea. God was looking out for her, too.

Offering: For a long time, I thought the story of Abraham and Isaac was about sacrificing everything for God. But after some study, I think it can be better framed as "what are you *unnecessarily* sacrificing for God?" Child sacrifice was very, very common in those days, and that's not how God rolls.

A psalm of david: Ruth was David's great-grandmother, and I enjoyed writing a poem where she was still alive when he was a boy.

Fruit trees for the fearful: See Joel 2:25–26.

www.ingramcontent.com/pod-product-compliance
Lightning Source LLC
Chambersburg PA
CBHW030851090426
42737CB00009B/1183